A Very Young Rider

Also by Jill Krementz

A Very Young Rider

Written and Photographed by
Jill Krementz

Library of Congress Cataloging in Publication Data

Krementz, Jill
A very young rider
1. Show riding—Juvenile literature.
2. Horses—Juvenile literature.
(1. Show riding. 2. Horses)
I. Title
SF294.7.K7S   798'.23   77-1996
ISBN 0-9755516-2-0

Manufactured in the United States of America

Graphics were directed by R.D. Schudellari; book design and
layout by Elissa Ichiyasu.

For my parents,
Virginia and Walter Krementz,
——— *with love* ———

Foreword by George H. Morris

A VERY YOUNG RIDER has special meaning for me. I knew Vivi Malloy and her family very well: she trained at Hunterdon with Jonathan Devine (now Soresi), who was my assistant at the time, and her older sister Debby was one of my students. They were enthusiastic and talented horsewomen, and as you will read in the article in the back of this edition of the book, horses have continued to play an important part of their lives.

Looking at Jill Krementz's wonderful photographs brings back so many memories of the "golden years" of American horse showing: my teacher and mentor Gordon Wright and another equally influential USET coach Bert de Nemethy; my own hero Bill Steinkraus; teammates Kathy Kusner and Frank Chapot; the great professional rider Rodney Jenkins; and Buddy Brown, one of my students who went on to Olympics success. And seeing them at the old National Horse Show at Madison Square Garden and Debby riding in the Maclay Finals there… could the 1970s be that long ago?

But *A VERY YOUNG RIDER* is much more than a nostalgic photo album. We also see Vivi grooming and exercising her pony Ready Penny, mucking out Penny's stall, and observing and learning from the pony's veterinarian and farrier. Such hands-on participation was all part of a rider's life in those days (but unfortunately less so today), and this book reminds us that it takes more than winning blue ribbons to become a complete horseman or horsewoman.

A VERY YOUNG RIDER had been out of print for many years. Now that it is once again available gives a new generation of pony riders the chance to meet Vivi and Penny, while we "old-timers" can again leaf through its pages and smile as we remember the way things were.

I don't know if I'll ever make the United States Equestrian Team when I grow up, but I really want to. I started riding when I was three. I'm ten now. My name is Vivi Malloy. My pony's name is Ready Penny. She's a chestnut and I've had her for two years. I ride her in horse shows in the medium pony hunter division.

She's 13.1 hands high. A hand is four inches, and you measure a horse from the ground to its withers. That's the place at the base of the neck where the mane starts. A large pony can be as tall as 14.2 hands. After that it's a horse and you can't show it in pony classes.

My older sister Debby has two horses. She's seventeen and she's ridden in the Maclay Finals in Madison Square Garden for the past three years. That's the big junior equitation class over fences. She's hoping to qualify again this year.

My brother Mark is thirteen and he rides in quite a few shows too. All three of us are very active in the Pony Club. The Pony Club is a nationwide organization that runs all kinds of instructional and competitive activities for children seventeen and under and their ponies. It's really fun.

Mom used to ride a lot when she was my age and she still goes fox hunting. Most of the time she helps Debby, Mark, and me with our riding.

The nonriders in the family are Dad and my other brothers, Andrew and Kenneth. They like football, golf, skiing, and swimming much more than horses. Sometimes they come and watch us when we're in horse shows, but that's mainly because Mom talks them into it.

I wish I could ride all the time, but of course I have to go to school during the day. My favorite subject is math.

The first thing I do when I get home is to run and say hello to Penny. She's usually outside in the paddock if it's warm. When it's cold, she stays in her stall.

As soon as we're finished saying hello, I go back to the barn and muck out her stall. Mucking out is a daily chore, like making your bed. Penny's bed has to be warm and dry or she'll get thrush, which is a very bad foot disease. I have to take out the manure with a pitchfork and remove the wet bedding. Then I turn over all the bedding and smooth it down. After the stall is clean, I go back to the paddock and get Penny.

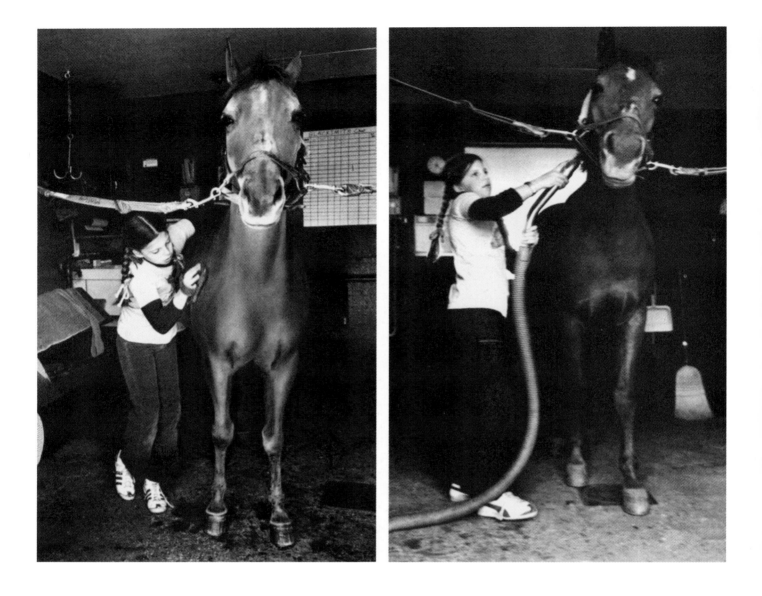

I bring her into the barn and put her on cross-ties. Then I start grooming her. First I use the curry comb to loosen the dirt and the long hairs on her coat. Then I vacuum her all over. This must tickle because Penny always flicks her ears when I do it.

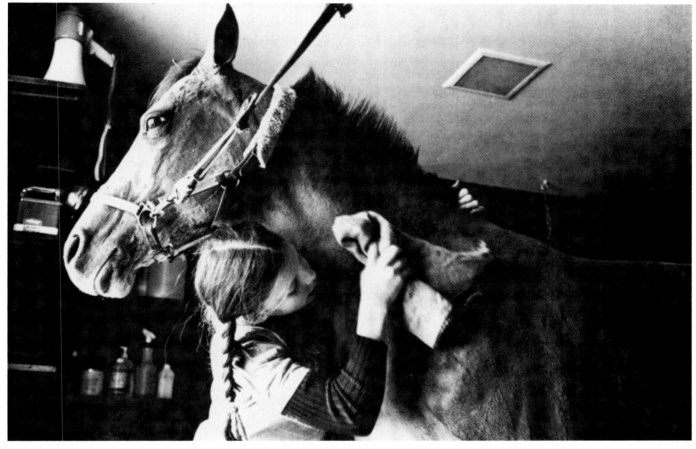

After that I use the body brush to get all her hair to lie flat and be shiny. Next step is to go all over her with a rub rag. Then I use the hoof pick because there could be some little stones stuck in her hoofs and that's bad. Last of all I treat her hoofs to keep them from getting dry and cracking. All this grooming takes about thirty minutes.

Then I put on my riding helmet, boots, and chaps. It's really dangerous to ride with sneakers because your foot can slide all the way through the stirrup and your ankle can get caught in the stirrup iron. The heel of a boot prevents this. The boots also protect your toes in case a horse steps on you. But not much.

After I'm dressed, I tack up Penny. She doesn't mind when I put the bridle on, but she doesn't like it when I tighten her girth. The girth is a leather strap that goes around her stomach and keeps the saddle on firmly. If it's not snug, the saddle slips.

Mom usually gives me a leg up. You always mount from the left because in medieval times knights wore their swords on their left side.

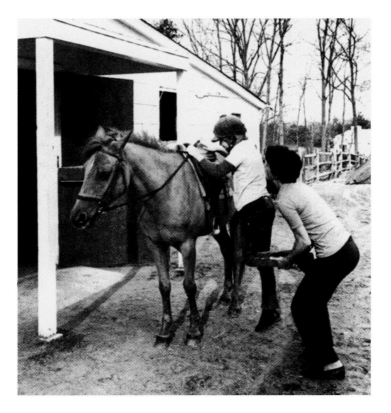

Behind the barn there's a riding ring. I ride for about an hour and practice my equitation, which means horsemanship. Good equitation is riding in the right position — your form, your style, and the way you fit your pony. It's very hard for me to keep my heels down so I work on that.

I show in the pony hunter division, which means that it's Penny's way of moving that's being judged, and not my equitation, but if my equitation isn't good, she won't look good either. Sometimes I ride in equitation classes so I won't get rusty.

What I try to work on is lightening my hands and sitting properly. People with heavy hands pull on the reins and that's very hard on a horse's mouth. Good hands are important because it's your hands that guide your horse.

I like jumping the best and so does Penny.

About once a week I have a lesson with Jonathan Devine. He works as an assistant for George Morris, who is Debby's trainer. George is really famous and all the best riders train with him. He used to be on the United States Equestrian Team, which represents the United States at the Olympics. He rode with the jumping team which won the Silver Medal in the 1960 Olympics in Rome. He doesn't train ponies though, so I'll have to wait until I'm older and bigger before I can train with him. But I really like training with Jonathan because he's teaching me the same system that George teaches Debby.

Jonathan is as serious about working on the flat as about jumping. He teaches me basic dressage—things like side-stepping, which is making the horse move from side to side. Napoleon, for instance, was very good at controlling his horse—if his horse acted up, he could always straighten it out. At horse shows we have classes where they judge us on the way our ponies walk, trot, and canter on the flat.

You make your horse move forward by squeezing the horse's sides with the calves of your legs. But if you squeeze with only one leg, the horse will move sideways, away from that leg. This is called leg yielding.

Jonathan also teaches a group of us at a nearby indoor riding ring.

About half of the lesson is on the flat and half is jumping.

After I finish riding, whether it's practicing by myself or having a lesson, there's quite a lot of work to be done. I have to cool out Penny and clean her up. I walk her for fifteen minutes without the saddle and with a wool cooler over her. This keeps her from getting a chill.

It's very important that you know these things because it's bad if a horse gets a cold. It's different from getting any old sniffle.

Horses have a very delicate digestive system — it was designed for a grass-eating animal. Also, they moved around a lot on the plains when they were wild. We give them concentrated feed and keep them stabled. Anything upsetting, like getting a chill, or eating or drinking too much when they're hot, can affect their digestive system and give them what is called colic. Colic is like a bad stomach ache. If horses get colic, it's really dangerous because they can die.

Sometimes, when it's hot outside, we give Penny a bath. If I've jumped her, I rub liniment on her legs and bandage them with flannel and cotton. When she's all clean I take her to her stall. If it's chilly I put a sheet on her.

Then I feed her dinner. First I give her hay. Hay is like an appetizer, like a salad before a meal.

Next I mix up her feed. She gets two quarts of sweet feed, two quarts of oats, and vitamins.

And I make sure she has plenty of water. Water is the most important. A horse can drink five to fifteen gallons of water a day.

After everyone's been hayed down and fed, we close the stall doors and say good-night.

We all help out with weekly barn duties. Debby and I usually scrub the buckets while Mark loads fresh bedding for the stalls. Most people think of straw as the usual bedding for horses but we use sawdust instead. It's cheaper and just as good.

Mark and I take turns raking the ring and that's the most fun. We have to do this or else the horses will get rocks in their feet. We all take turns brushing away the cobwebs.

One thing I'm *very* involved with is Pony Club. Sometimes on weekends, or during vacations from school, we go on field trips to breeding farms or other people's stables. These trips are called unmounted meetings. One time we went to Mrs. Debany's farm to see a new foal who was only one week old. He was born three weeks prematurely so he was very tiny. He weighed about seventy-five pounds. They named him Grasshopper. Mrs. Debany told us that the mother of a newborn is very protective, particularly the first week, because she feels she can take care of her foal better than people can. She probably can, too. She'll keep her foal moving as much as possible the first week so it will develop its muscles and get strong. Moving around also helps get the mare's figure back after giving birth. Mares carry for approximately eleven months. They go to a lot of trouble to give birth when no one's looking. The birth only takes about ten minutes.

After the newborn foal is up on its feet, the mother licks it dry. I don't understand how you can lick something dry but cats and horses do it.

A girl is called a filly and a boy is a colt.

A foal can run and keep up with its mother when it's only twenty-four hours old.

On a hot day, when the flies are out, a foal will usually stand next to its mother's tail to take advantage of the swishing. They sure are smart.

It's called a foal until it's weaned, which is in about six months. Then it's called a weanling until it's a year old. Then it's called a yearling. After that they're called two-year-olds, three-year-olds, and so on. Horses can live to be as old as thirty. Ponies usually live a little longer.

Some people think that ponies will grow up to become horses but that isn't so. A pony's foal grows up to be a pony and a horse's foal grows up to be a horse.

Our vet's name is Bill Bradley. He has a special truck, which is refrigerated and has hot and cold running water and an X-ray machine. He comes routinely for things like worming and giving shots, but makes special trips to sign a health certificate for an out-of-state horse show or if one of the horses gets sick.

About twice a year he files down Penny's teeth. This is called floating the teeth. Horses have to have smooth teeth in order to chew their grain. As they chew, their teeth can wear down and form sharp edges which cut their cheeks and tongue. When this happens, they don't chew their food properly and then they have trouble digesting. Penny hates having her teeth floated, and sometimes she puts up a big argument. Dr. Bradley says that he and Penny get along a lot better than they used to.

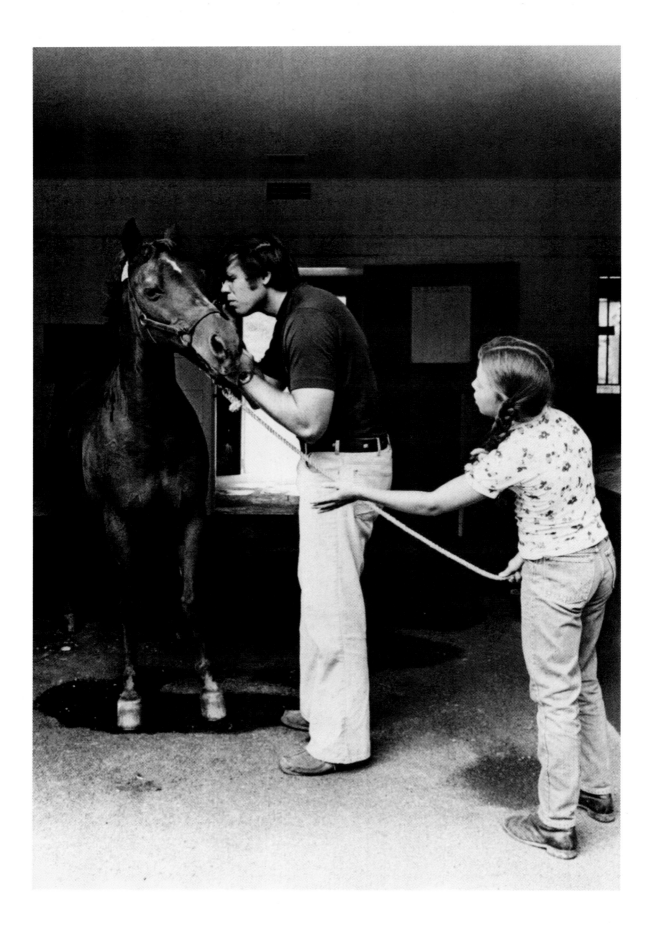

During a regular checkup, he looks at Penny's eyes to be sure her vision is normal.

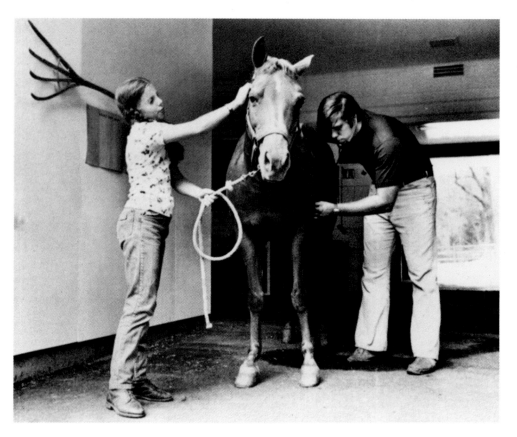

He also listens to her heart and lungs and checks her legs for lameness.

About five years ago Debby thought she wanted to be a vet, so she used to tag along with Dr. Bradley when he went to his different appointments. She really knows what to do when a horse gets cut or a cat gets stepped on. I wouldn't mind being a vet, except for doing operations. I can't stand operations. I think I'd rather be a trainer.

Once a month the farrier comes to shoe all the horses. Or, if a horse throws a shoe, he makes a special trip. His name is Michael Lynch and he's been in the business about thirty years. His father was a farrier and taught him how to do it. It's important to get a farrier who knows what he's doing because a bad one can do real damage to a horse. There are a lot of bad ones because they don't have to take a test or have a license.

The word "farrier" comes from England and means horse-shoe-er. The farrier takes care of the horses' feet only. Lots of people call them blacksmiths by mistake. A blacksmith is the person who does the iron work, which means the steel shaping and the forging. Sometimes Mr. Lynch brings a blacksmith with him but lots of times he does both jobs by himself.

First he takes off the horse's shoes and trims down the hoofs. They grow just like a person's toenails and it's very bad for the horse if they get too big. If their hoofs grow too much, they get clumsy and it can make them lame. It's like wearing a shoe that's too big for you.

After the hoofs are pared down, Mr. Lynch sets up the forge. It has a fan that blows under a fire and gives off very concentrated heat. He puts the shoes in the fire and gets them hot so they get soft and he can bend and shape them. This takes about five minutes after the fire's warmed up and really going.

As each shoe gets red hot, he puts it on an anvil and shapes it with a hammer to fit the horse's foot. When the shoes are cool, Mr. Lynch nails them on. The nails are wedge-shaped so that when you drive them in they come out the side of the hoof. He bends the nails over and files them down. The average shoe gets six nails but there are eight holes if you need that many. A pony like Penny only needs six.

Shoeing doesn't hurt the horse at all if it's done right. Sometimes it hurts the farrier because the horse gets nervous and bites or kicks him. Mr. Lynch has had to go to the hospital lots of times with cracked ribs.

The reason horses need shoes is the same reason people need them—to protect their feet. American Indians used to cover the horses' hoofs with hides from other animals when they took them through mountain areas, over stones. They would tie the hides up around the horses' ankles, just the way they tied their own moccasins.

We go to The Saddler in Wilton, Connecticut, to get stuff repaired and to get riding clothes. Mom also gets presents for our birthdays there. They have all kinds of riding clothes for people: jodhpurs, britches, jackets, hats, boots, shirts, stocks, ties, chokers, and things like garter straps, spurs, and gloves. And for horses they have all kinds of tack: saddles, bridles, and halters, and equipment like sheets, saddle pads, and lead and lunge lines. In fact, they have everything for taking care of a horse, even fly sprays, hoof oil, saddle soap, and ointments for cuts.

When you buy a jacket or jodhpurs, they have you sit on a saddle to see how everything will fit when you're sitting on a horse. When you get boots, they have to measure your feet and your legs too. Mr. Aquino, who owns The Saddler, does the fitting. I get bigger boots than my size to have some growing room.

What I love the most is competing in horse shows around the country. I compete in about fifteen major shows a year—in spring, summer, and fall. I don't show in the winter because most of the good showing is in Florida and I have to be in school.

Showing takes a lot of time, especially getting ready. Before each show I have to clean my tack…clean it really well. First, I clean the leather of my saddle and bridle with saddle soap—this keeps the leather moist so it doesn't crack and break. Then I polish the metal parts of my bridle: the bit, the rings, and all the buckles. Mom says I'm good at that.

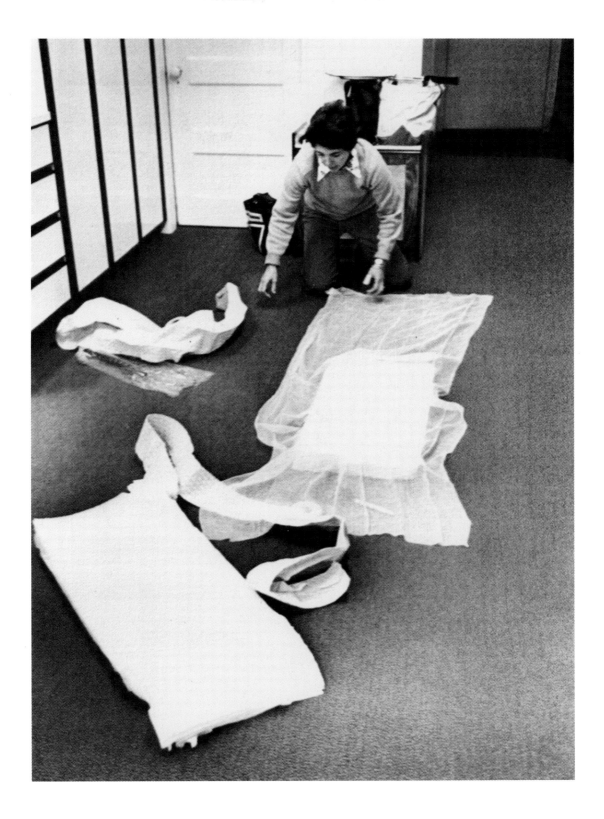

Mom makes the shipping bandages for the horses' legs. They protect the horses' legs in shipping when they're in the van and trying to keep their balance. Once Mark and Debby and I got in the back of the van on our hands and knees and Mom drove around so that we'd know what it feels like for the horses. It was very bumpy and we had to keep our balance by shifting our weight. And it was scary not being able to see where we were going.

In the spring, when I'm still in school, most of the horse shows I compete in are on weekends. The first big show of the spring season is Boulder Brook, in the beginning of April. Boulder Brook is near where we live so we don't have to stay in a motel.

The night before a show I try to get to bed early. I set the alarm for around four a.m. I love waking up when it's pitch black outside. You're awake before the whole world and there are no noises — no sounds at all. It's so neat.

Before I go to sleep, I put out the clothes I'll be wearing and I write in my diary.

We van Penny over in the morning. The back of the van has a stall where we can keep her between classes. It's like her home away from home.

I have my own time schedule, which tells me when to have Penny ready for her classes and which ring we're showing in. My brother Mark usually comes along to work as the groom.

The program tells me the class regulations, the judges, and the names of the other competitors. I always look to see which of my friends are showing. It also lists all the different divisions and the ribbons and prizes for each class.

About a half-hour before the class is scheduled to start, I go up to the ring and find Jonathan.

Then I wait with him until it's my turn to compete. He usually reminds me not to get nervous and just to concentrate on the course.

The hunter course consists of a variety of eight jumps. There are usually several post and rails, a gate, a wall, and an in-and-out. We have to jump them in a certain order. They usually display a diagram of the course near the ring. I watch the other horses in the ring and decide how many strides it takes to get from one fence to another. If I'm first in the ring, Jonathan calculates it for me. I hate being first.

Penny and I won quite a few ribbons at Boulder Brook. It's important to be in the ribbons early in the year so that you can qualify for the really big summer shows like Lake Placid and Devon, and the fall shows at Harrisburg and Washington, D.C. You have to have a certain number of points just to enter these shows.

I won some money too. When I win money, I give Mom half to cover my entrance fees and I put the rest into my savings account.

There are six to ten ribbons awarded in each class depending on the show. A blue ribbon, which is the first prize, is assigned five points; a red ribbon, which is second, is three points; yellow, which is third, gets two points; and a white ribbon, which is fourth prize, gets one point. All your points are added up from each class that you win and at the end of the show the horse with the most points in each division is the champion.

Later this spring Penny was the champion at Syracuse, which means she got the highest number of points in her class. They gave us a cooler that said "Pony Champion—Syracuse Horse Show."

During summer, when school's out, we travel to a lot of outdoor shows. They're very fancy and have lots of prestige. Since we're away for a week at a time, we have to pack a tack trunk of stuff like coolers, fly sheets, and grooming equipment.

Last summer we went to Farmington, Devon, Ox Ridge, Fairfield, and Lake Placid. We also went to a few shows on Long Island—Southampton, C. W. Post, and North Shore. Mom or Debby drives the van. When we get to the show grounds, they assign us temporary stalls. They're in big tents and it almost looks like a circus.

As soon as we arrive at the show grounds, I take Penny for a walk to stretch her legs.

When a rider and a pony have been working together for a long time, they kind of develop a language.

After the horses are comfortable and in their stalls, we set up our tack trunk and put up our tack room hangings.

Then we buy a few bales of straw for Penny's bedding and a few bales of hay for her dinner. Penny gets one or two flakes of hay depending on how hard I'm working her. A flake is part of a bale.

I love staying at motels. It's so much fun. Sometimes I can share a room with a friend like Amy Weiss. We play games like "Twenty Questions" and stuff like that. Mom's in a connecting room so we can't be too loud. We get to go out for dinner every night. I like to try different foods that I've never heard of. I also get to watch TV in bed. I like "The Bionic Woman."

On the days we are showing, we try to get to the show grounds around five a.m. because there's a lot to do. First I feed, hay, and water Penny.

Then I get right down to braiding. In olden times horses were braided for the hunt field so their manes and tails wouldn't get tangled in the brambles when they went galloping through the woods. Nowadays it is done for hunter classes to make a horse look fancy and show off its neck and hindquarters.

Sometimes Kym helps. He's a professional braider and can do it a lot faster than I can. He can do about twelve horses a day. Some of the older girls who are showing do braiding to earn extra money.

Braiding tails is not the same as braiding pigtails. It's much harder. Penny's tail is especially hard to do because she has a crooked tail bone.

If it's a rainy day, we do a mud tail. That's when the hairs that normally hang down are doubled up and woven into the braid so they don't get muddy. I *hate* showing in the rain and Penny hates it even more. She actually makes a bad face when she goes out in the rain.

After Penny is braided, I work her on the lunge line for about twenty minutes.

Lungeing exercises her when she's away from home and can't go out and run.

I make her walk, trot, and canter at the end of the line.

Around seven I go and find Jonathan and we school Penny over the jumps she'll have to jump that day. They usually let us practice in the ring. Jonathan goes over the course with me and asks me if I feel all right for the show. We practice the distances between the fences. Then I go back to the tent and wash down Penny. I let her graze for a while.

Next I go up and get my order, which is posted at the gate. They pick the first number for the first class out of a hat. They give you a different order for each class. I like to ride in the middle so I can watch the first people and judge the distances, and then go before the course gets all churned up with hoofprints. They announce the beginning of each class over the loudspeaker—it's called a stable call. There's a thirty-minute call and then a fifteen-minute call.

After I know my order, I like to relax and play checkers with Matthew Burdsall until my first class. When I go into the ring I put a lot of pressure on myself so it's important to take it easy beforehand.

Matthew is my age and rides in most of the shows. He trains with his sister, Katherine. She won the Maclay Finals in Madison Square Garden last year. She's seventeen. Matthew has been riding for a little over a year. Boys usually start riding later than girls. Mom thinks it's because they don't like taking care of horses until they get a little bit older.

As soon as I hear the ringmaster's horn, I know the show is about to start.

Honey Craven was the ringmaster at Devon this year. He's been the ringmaster at Devon and the National Horse Show in Madison Square Garden for umpteen years.

Just before my first class, Mom rebraids my hair. I should be able to do it myself since I can braid Penny's mane, but I'm not very good at it. Mom says I should practice on rainy days. I always wear green and white ribbons because they're my lucky colors.

We get our numbers in the horse show office. You wear the same number throughout the show.

I always wear my Pony Club pin on my riding helmet. You get it when you join.

About ten minutes before I go into the ring, Jonathan goes over the course with me one more time. Then I warm up in the schooling area next to the ring for about five minutes. This time is very important because I find out what kind of mood my pony's in and I get used to jumping. It's like in baseball when the pitcher goes into the warm-up cage or when the batter swings a few bats. I have to get really used to finding the distance or place for my pony to leave the ground.

I love the schooling area at Lake Placid the best because the trees are so beautiful.

When the paddock master calls my number the first time, I know I only have a few minutes before my round. They call you three times in all. The first gets you up near the ring. The second is for you to get on deck. And the third is to enter the ring. They have a one-minute rule. If you're not in the ring within one minute after they call your number the third time, you're eliminated. That's never happened to me.

Jonathan gives me last-minute instructions except when I'm nervous and then he leaves me alone.

While I'm on deck, Mom touches up Penny's hoofs with hoof oil.

Then I wait in the starting gate for my number to be called the final time.

Jonathan always watches me and sometimes George Morris does too.

The person who's watching me the closest is the judge. Charles Dennehy is from Lake Forest, Illinois, and he judges many of the top shows throughout the country.

I love the schooling and all the practice, but what I love most is the moment in the ring when you have to give it your all.

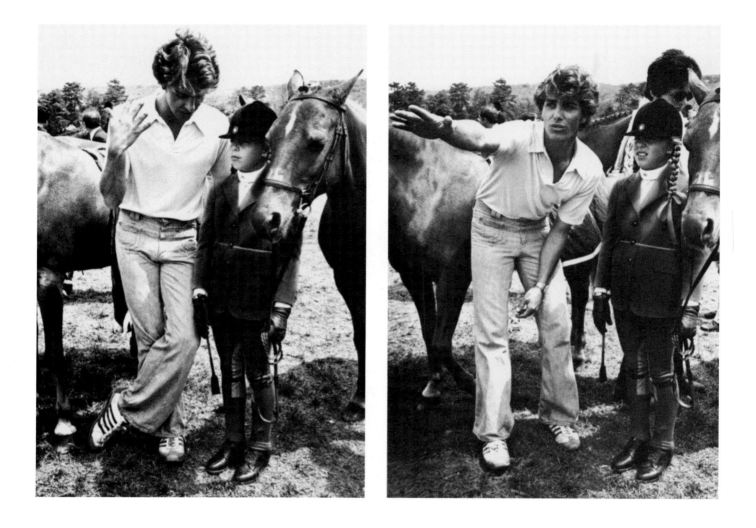

After I finish in the ring, I dismount and Jonathan comes right over to tell me what I could have done better. Once in a while he says it was perfect, but not very often.

After everyone has ridden in the class, they call back the ten ponies who've had the best rounds to the center of the ring. They do this to make sure the ponies are sound in case someone has jumped a lame pony. Lameness doesn't really show when they're jumping but when they're jogged out for soundness it will.

Then they award the ribbons.

If you win, one of the show photographers usually takes your picture. George Axt has been taking pictures at horse shows for twenty years. He lives in a camper and travels to all the shows. He also takes video tapes of people riding. He develops and prints right in his trailer. He has a funny hat that he throws into the air to make the horses put their ears forward.

Although most of my classes are pony hunter, where Penny's being judged, I usually ride in one or two equitation classes on the flat. In those classes they are judging *my* form. We all go into the ring at the same time and the judge makes us walk, trot, and canter. Then there are certain individual tests that the judge can ask of his top choices before he makes his final decision. The ringmaster always says, "Don't bunch together—spread out!" But we always *do* bunch up.

Debby did very well this year. She rides in the junior jumper classes. These are classes that are judged on how high and how fast her horse can jump and maneuver a small tight course. My pony hunter classes are judged on how evenly I can jump my eight fences. Debby's fences can go up to five feet but mine can't be higher than two and a half feet.

I love it if I happen to be nearby when George talks to Debby about riding.

Debby and I usually try and watch each other's rounds if we don't have classes at the same time, and then we can talk about how we thought they went. Sometimes if I feel discouraged, Debby tells me that she made the same mistakes when she was my age.

One of the most exciting parts of the horse show circuit is getting to see the famous riders like Rodney Jenkins. I can learn a lot just watching him school his horses.

I really like Rodney. He's been riding since he was seven and now he's a professional. Sometimes he rides his own horse but mostly he rides other people's for them.

I got his autograph this year at Devon.

They always have a lead-line class at Devon. It's for little kids who are usually going into the show ring for the first time and it's very funny. I was in the lead-line classes five years ago on my first pony, called Fifi. She was a chestnut Shetland pony and she was only eight hands high.

At the end of the class everyone got lollypops.

When I'm not in classes or watching the show, I like to go around with my friend Meg Brown. Her older brother, Buddy, is on the United States Olympic Team. Meg usually rides her pony but this summer she couldn't because her pony had just foaled. Her family has a trailer, which they live in when they're on the road showing.

I love cotton candy but it's so fattening. When I get older like Debby, I'll have to go on a diet. Debby's always on a diet or else George gets after her. Once she went on a pure liquid diet and almost fainted in school. I have to watch my weight now a little bit. You don't want to get too heavy for your pony. There's nothing uglier than a fat rider on a horse. It's important to eat a lot of vitamins and protein to keep your energy up.

There's a man named Seaweed who goes to all the horse shows, starting with Florida in the winter. His specialty is bacon and egg sandwiches. He sells a lot of cheeseburgers too. At Ox Ridge he sold 10,000. He used to be a good rider. He also works on the jump crew putting up jumps. And sometimes he even runs the gate.

Each day at a show is a little different, but I always finish up by cleaning my tack and mucking out the stall.

Then I feed Penny, and Mom and I head back to the motel for a good night's sleep before another day of showing.

By the middle of August most of the summer shows are over. Both Debby and I did well this summer. Debby qualified for the Maclay Finals and we both qualified for Harrisburg and Washington, D.C.

They send you a notice of acceptance in the mail.

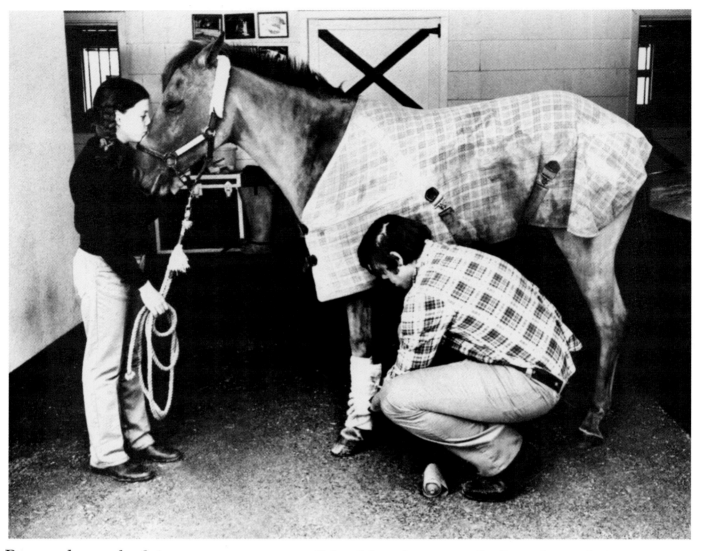

But at the end of August, a most terrible thing happened! One day while we were schooling, Penny went lame. Dr. Bradley came over and said that she had hurt her tendon. He bandaged her leg with a gel cast and gave her a shot. He said that her leg needed complete rest and that I couldn't ride her for at least a few months. I felt awful.

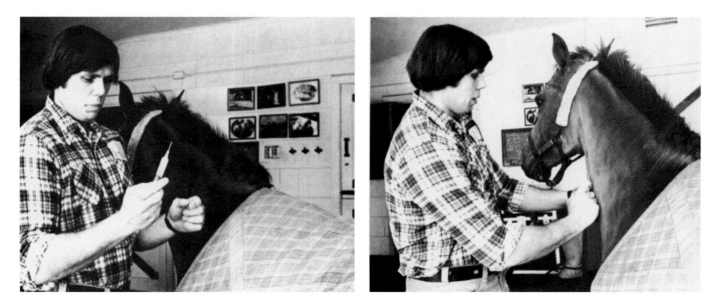

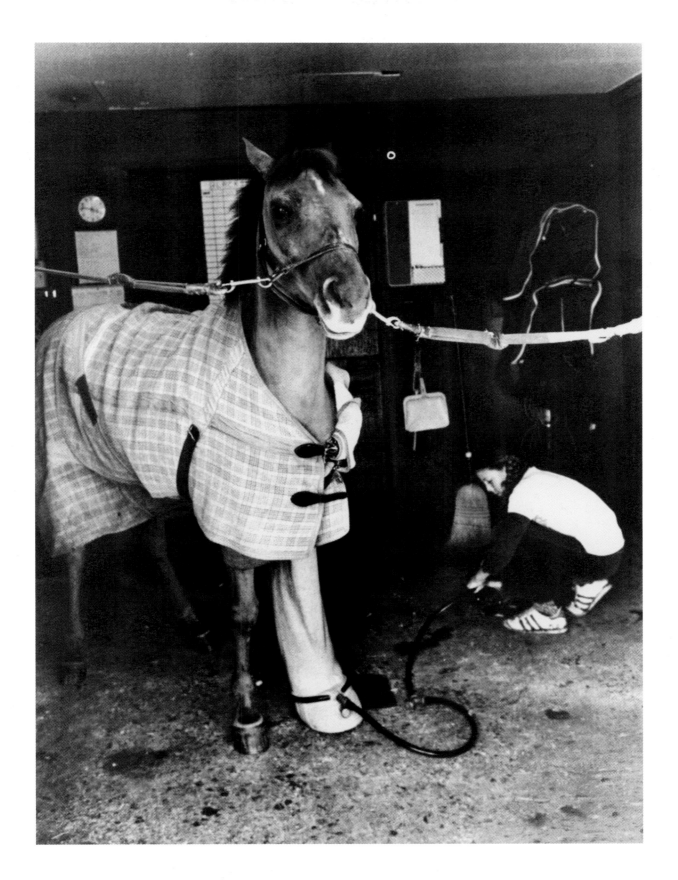

Dr. Bradley took off the cast in a few days and I gave her a whirlpool treatment every day for several weeks. She made wonderful progress and finally was good as new. Thank goodness! But I still couldn't take her to Harrisburg or Washington.

Once a year, in August, there's a Pony Club rally and I'd also been looking forward to riding Penny in that. Since she was lame, I borrowed another pony from friends.

Each region has its own rally. Debby, Mark, and I are members of the Greenwich Pony Club, which is part of the Metropolitan Region. It's the only time in riding that I compete as part of a team instead of as an individual. We ride in a team, the same way they do at the Olympics. Each team competes in a number of events: dressage, cross country, and stadium jumping. The team that gets the most points wins. Unlike riders in the Olympics, we have to take a written test and we're also judged on stable management.

Mark was our captain and the other members of our team were Joan Levee and Jimmy Kingery. Mark kept complaining that it was hard to be captain of us kids because we never listened to him.

The rally only lasts one day and starts around eight in the morning. Mom was the rally coordinator and Jack Graham was the overall judge. The rally begins with a call to order. We're told that before any of the events, we'll have an inspection of our vans and tack. No one is allowed to help us or even talk to us, or we get points taken off.

My favorite event is cross country because you go out by yourself and have to ride over rough terrain. You have to get to the finish line within a certain number of minutes or you're eliminated. The time allowed is usually very fast so the ride is always exciting. Debby was one of the official judges making a safety check at the starting line. This is the final check over all the tack to make sure it's adjusted properly, is clean and in good condition.

When I was ready to go, the timekeeper recorded my starting time. I had a clear run and I finished in nine minutes. They have judges posted at all the jumps in the woods. If your horse refuses a jump, they mark down a fault on their score cards.

After the summer is over, it's back to school. The horses get a good rest and we all take a breather before Debby gets ready for Madison Square Garden in November.

We usually clean and repaint all the tack trunks.

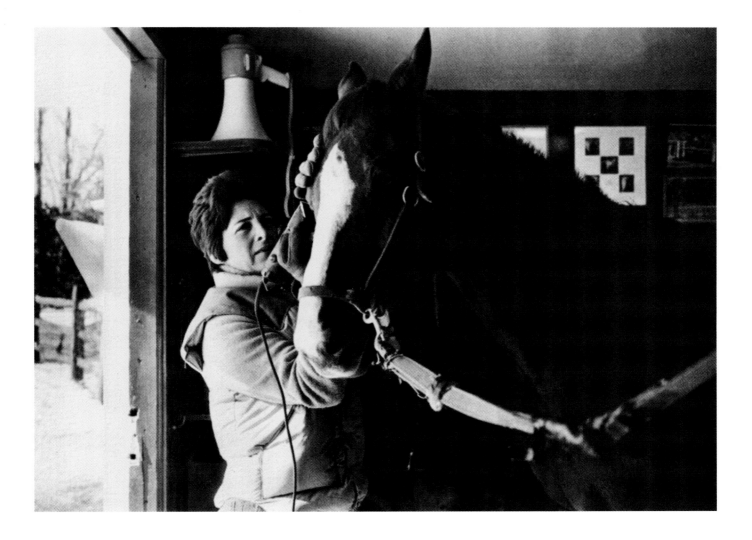

We also have to clip Debby's horse because you can't show a horse with a shaggy coat in the Garden.

The National in the Garden is the most exciting horse show of all! This year I went to the opening night with Jonathan. He was all dressed up. The show lasts for a week and there are classes all day and then more at night. Mom usually lets me take a day or two off from school because it only happens once a year.

Lots of famous horse people come to watch. I saw Kathy Kusner, who is one of my idols. She made the United States Equestrian Team when she was twenty-one and rode in the Olympics three times. Then she became a steeplechase jockey. She got her first pony when she was twelve years old and used to sell pony rides on him so he could be self-supporting. I also saw Bert de Nemethy, who is the coach of the U.S.E.T. Gordon Wright was there too. He trained George Morris, William Steinkraus, and lots of other famous riders. He still teaches but not as much as he used to.

Victor Hugo-Vidal, a very famous rider and trainer, is always the main announcer.

There was a big marching band, which was very loud. The whole Garden was draped with bunting and flags from all the nations competing in the international classes.

Then there was a parade of teams. The United States Equestrian Team has four members—Frank Chapot, who is captain, Michael Matz, Buddy Brown, and Dennis Murphy. When each team rode out, the band played its national anthem. This year there were seven international teams and they came from Australia, Belgium, Canada, Holland, Ireland, Puerto Rico, and the United States. A team can have one to four members.

It would be so exciting to ride with the U.S.E.T. There aren't any women on the team now but there have been quite a few in the past. I hope I can make it when I grow up.

One of my favorite events was an exhibition by the Royal Canadian Mounted Police. I love to watch them perform. They do all kinds of maneuvers, with names like "Clover Leaf" and "Threading the Needle," in time to music. While we were watching, Jonathan explained to me that even though the drills looked very complicated, they were all made up of separate dressage movements he and I had worked on together.

The horses are all matched bays and each one has a maple leaf stenciled on its hindquarters. This is done by laying the stencil of the leaf on its rump and brushing the hair the wrong way with a wet brush.

And all of the horses' manes are clipped except for one. That's the horse that Queen Elizabeth rides when she visits Canada.

The Mounties wear ceremonial scarlet tunics and carry lances.

I counted thirty-two of them.

Buddy Brown rode throughout the week and I got to watch him a lot. He's the youngest rider on the team.

This year the United States won the Nations Cup for the fifth time, which means they get to keep the trophy. Buddy won quite a few ribbons.

Afterwards I went back to the stabling area to see him.

On Saturday afternoon Debby was one of eleven riders called into the middle of the ring. They were the high-point winners of the year in the Professional Horseman's Association Equitation Trophy. Victor Hugo-Vidal gave her a ribbon, a silver dish, and a kiss! The whole family came to the Garden, including my grandparents.

On the last day of the show, Debby rode in the Maclay Finals. There were 159 competitors from twenty-six states in her class. She didn't win anything but George told her she rode well and that's the most important thing. The girl who did win is another one of George's students. Her name is Colette Lozins and she's only sixteen years old. George won both the Maclay and the Medal when he was only fourteen. Nobody else has ever done that. Debby still has one more year to try for the title.

I hope I get to ride in the Garden some day.

After the Garden, Jonathan told me that I really should think about selling Penny because I was getting too big for her. I knew it was for my own good, but it made me very sad to think of saying goodbye to a pony I love.

Mom, Debby, and I went to see some bigger ponies. Mara Tarnapol, one of our neighbors, had a nice one. It was the perfect size for me, and I liked riding her a lot.

Another thing that happened was that Fifi, who was my very first pony, came home for a visit. Our neighbors have a little girl who is learning to ride on Fifi. I'm glad that the people who have her now live next door so I can see her sometimes.

Another family nearby—the Pedersens—wanted Penny for their little girl named Muffy. Muffy is smaller than I am and is just starting to show in pony classes. I took her for a ride on the lead line so she could try Penny out.

Afterwards we had a talk, and I told Muffy what Penny's feed is and the things she likes and doesn't like—such as how she loves to be scratched behind her ears.

Penny will be perfect for her. They will give Penny lots of love and the best of care.

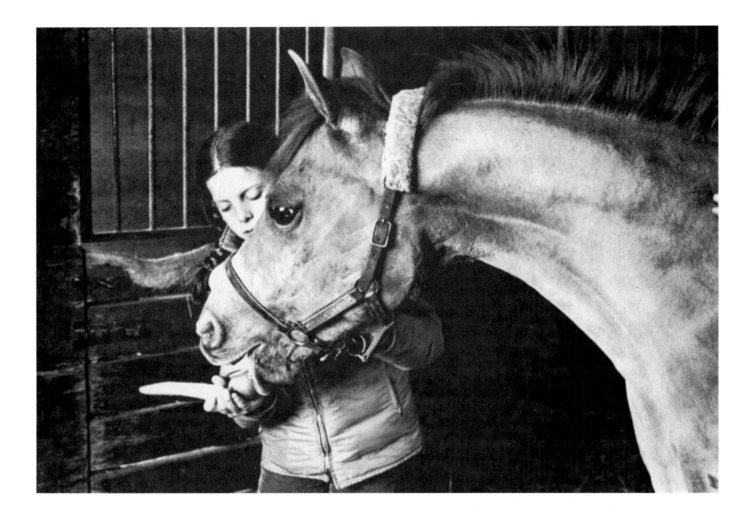

On the night before Penny left for her new home, I went down to the barn. I gave her some apples and carrots. I told her how much I loved her and that we would see each other in the spring at all the shows. And then I kissed her goodbye.

That night when I went to bed, I cried. Mom said that I shouldn't feel too sad because Penny was going to such a nice family and because Christmas was coming soon.

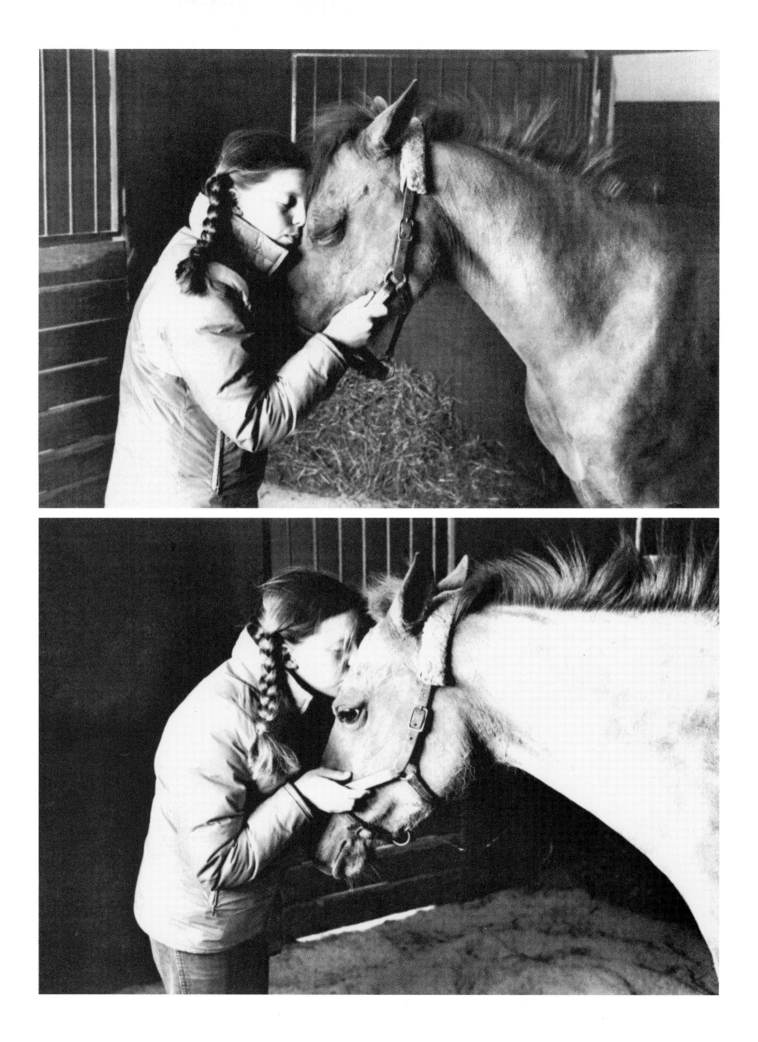

On Christmas morning Mom came into my room very early with two presents. Normally we all wait until after breakfast but Mom was so excited she couldn't wait.

I opened the first box and couldn't believe it. Inside was a brand new show halter and a note from Mom and Dad.

The note said: *"We couldn't fit your new pony into this box but she's waiting for you in the barn."*

Then she gave me a present from my grandparents...a beautiful green and white horse blanket with my initials on it.

I must have gotten dressed in two seconds. I ran down to the barn with the halter and blanket as fast as I could.

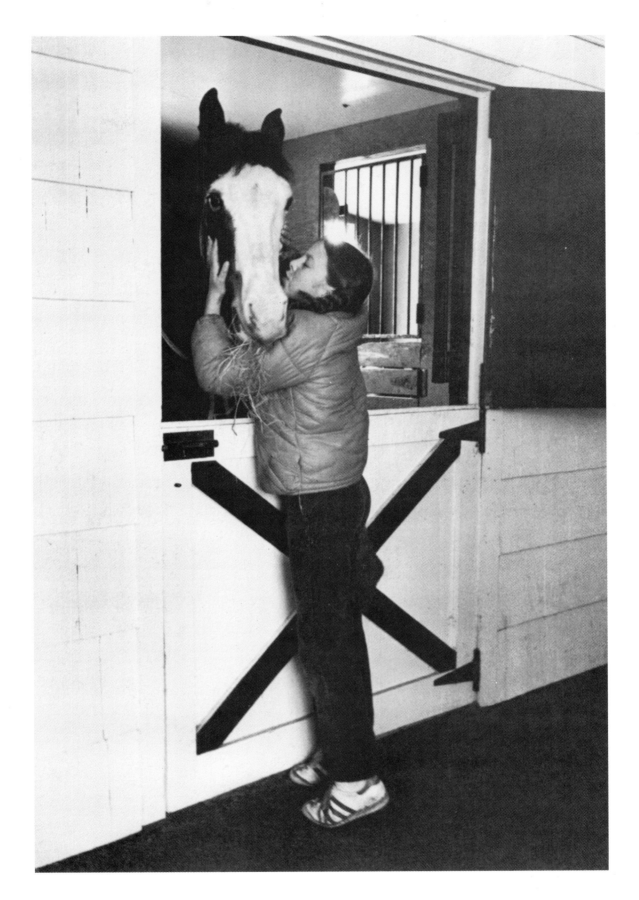

There was a new pony waiting for me in the stall. Of course I recognized her right away. She had a red ribbon tied around her neck. I ran up and gave her a big hug and a kiss. I could tell that we were going to get along together just fine.

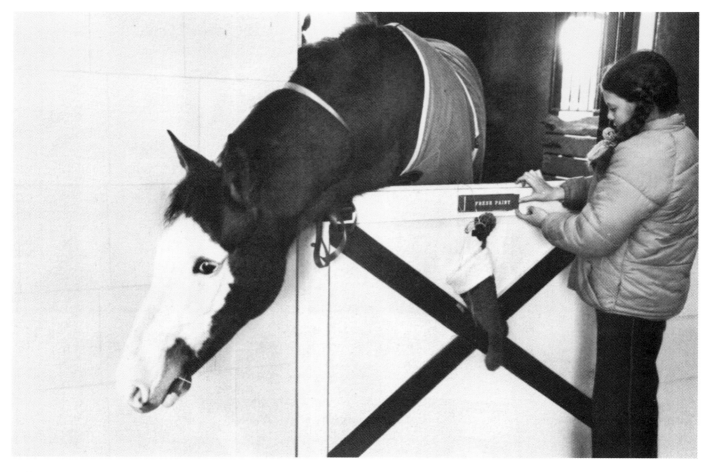

There was a new name plate in the slot on the door. It said "Fresh Paint." It's a perfect name for her because she looks as if she has a splash of white paint on her face.

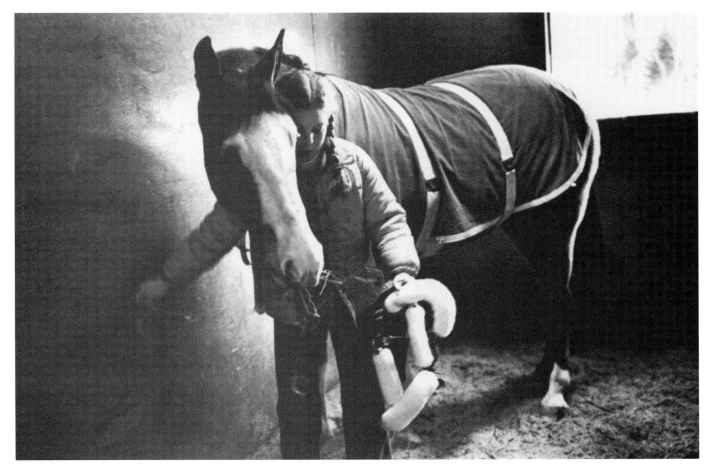

I put the new halter and blanket on her. Then I walked her outside and admired her. She's 14 hands, which means I'll show her in the large pony division.

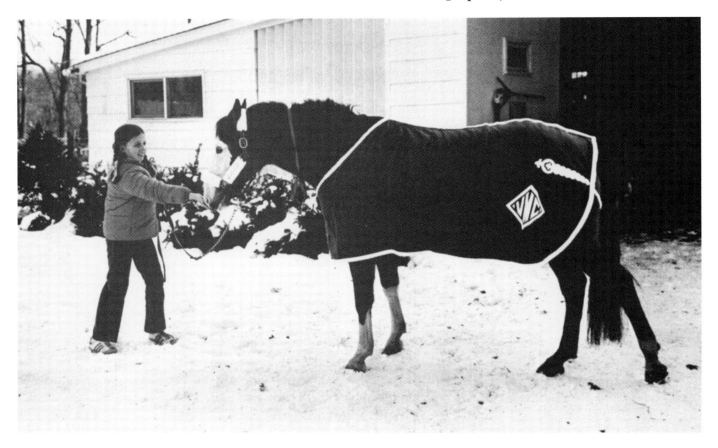

Mom and Dad came out to see us. I hugged them both and they helped me up on her.

Afterwards I took Paint, which is what I'll call her, for a little run in the snow. I told her what an exciting year we had ahead of us.

I hope we'll have as many good times together as Penny and I did.

A Very Young Rider Grows Up

*Like many horse-crazy girls, I grew up enjoying Jill Krementz'
book* A Very Young Rider, *starring Vivi Malloy. Almost 30
years later, the story still continues.*

Tricia Booker

It's hard to fathom the number of girls who've paged
through the book *A Very Young Rider*, published in 1977, and
dreamed of living the life of Vivi Malloy. Even now, with the
book out of print for many years, it's still a hot commodity on
eBay and considered a classic horse book for children.

In the photographically rich book published by Alfred
A. Knopf, written and photographed by Jill Krementz, the
reader tags along with 10-year-old Vivi on her daily life on
the A-rated horse show circuit as she trains, prepares and
shows her medium pony, Ready Penny. Her coach, Jonathan
Devine, a protégé of George Morris, and her older sister,
Debby, who also rides out of Hunterdon, are integral parts
of the story too.

I remember spending hours poring over the text and
photos when I was a child. I'd just started showing at
the rated shows in the children's hunter division and
was mesmerized by Vivi's story. I'd heard of many places
mentioned in the book, such as New York City's Madison
Square Garden, the ASPCA Maclay Finals and the Devon
Horse Show (Pa.), but until I picked up this book, I'd never
seen them.

Three years later, when I went to the Garden for the first
time, it looked so much like the photographs in the book.

So as the children of the '70s and '80s grew up, went
to college, started careers and married, many may have
stumbled across the book again at the library or even
have saved it for their own children. Some have probably
wondered, as I have, "What ever happened to Vivi Malloy?"

Well, at the close of the book, Vivi outgrows and sells
"Penny" and receives a surprise pony for Christmas named
Fresh Paint. She says on the last page, "I hope we'll have as
many good times together as Penny and I did."

And, she did, with many more horses playing starring
roles in her life too.

▶ A Child's Life

I caught up with Vivi by telephone as she vacationed
with her family in Barbados in late March. She's 39 now,
married to an attorney named Rich Hanson, and lives in
Chicago. Her two children, Owen, 3½, and Julia, 21
months, chirped in the background as we spoke about her
life after *A Very Young Rider* was published.

"It's been amazing," she said of the book. "There are
still little girls who write to me about the book—just every
once in awhile, but it's wonderful. The book still speaks to
kids. I like that it's timeless."

Vivi was 9 when Krementz started the project. They met
at a horse show, where Krementz was searching for the right
child to star in the book. She wanted a young girl who cared
for her own pony and found Vivi the perfect fit.

"I vaguely remember her taking photos of me at Boulder
Brook [N.Y.] one day. She followed me back to the van and
approached my mom then, and it went on from there. She
came to our home and took lots of photos and really planted
herself. That's her process. She gets into the whole routine
and can write honestly and on a child's level," said Vivi.

Krementz interviewed Vivi regularly and photographed
her at home, at shows, in hotels, and while schooling,
showing, mucking stalls, holding Penny for the veterinarian
and farrier, cleaning tack, and just about everything that
goes along with caring for a pony.

"She was a true professional photographer
and knew how to capture the nature of horses
respectfully," said Vivi. "She knew where she
needed to be."

Some have speculated over the years that the
final few pages, where Vivi received Fresh Paint for
Christmas, were fictionalized. But Vivi assured me
that the story was absolutely true.

"It was the only part of the book that was
recreated," she explained. "Jill didn't come over
on Christmas morning. But I did wake up on
Christmas and find a blanket at the foot of my bed
and a new pony in the barn."

After the book was published, Vivi remembers
it wasn't quite the same. "It felt strange to be the
center of attention. I was serious and committed
to riding, but I wasn't looking for people to
pay attention to me. As a 10-year-old, I didn't
understand the big deal. It was my life. I knew I
was lucky to ride horses, but it was just my life. At
the time I felt like, 'I'm not as good as so-and-so.
Why me?'

"But as the years have gone by it's been
gratifying. As I got older—and went off to college
at a large university—I stopped riding and moved
into another phase of my life. Then I understood
why little girls responded. I've come to realize
over the years how special it is. She chose me. She
could have chosen someone else just as easily. It
was just my story."

Vivi concluded her junior career aboard jumpers Reilly
and Apple Core and concentrated on equitation, as her
sister Debby had done. A highlight was third in the 1983
USET Medal Finals behind Karen McKelvy and Francesca
Mazella.

She continued riding for pleasure during her college
years while she focused on her education. She received her
undergraduate degree from the University of Michigan in
art history. After a stint working in New York City in the
publishing industry, Vivi returned to school and earned
her master's degree in social work from the University of
Chicago.

She then began working with children and families in a
community mental-health setting, dealing with issues like
developmental delays and family stress and trauma.

"It was very rewarding to help kids whose development
was compromised, to help them through it," she said.

Through her social-work connections she became a
volunteer at Equi-Therapy, in Morton Grove, Ill., where
she began working part-time. After the program's director
stepped down, she took over temporarily, until she became
pregnant with Owen.

"That was the most amazing experience," she said. "It
was a perfect marriage between my professional training and
what I was bred to do, being with the horses. It just felt so
natural. The idea of horses and therapeutic healing worked.
I'm planning to get back into it in the future."

▶ A Life Of Horses

Vivi's mother, Vivien Malloy, has become even more
immersed in horses since her five children—Andrew,
Debby, Kenneth, Mark and Vivi—have grown up. She and
husband Harry now run Edition Farm, in Hyde Park, N.Y.,
where they breed and race New York-bred Thoroughbreds.

"When all of the children left to get married or go to
college, I inherited Vivi's equitation horse. I did the adult
equitation and showed, but I had always wanted to breed
horses," Vivien said.

So Vivien asked a friend to help her find a broodmare,
and that single mare, in foal with a foal at her side, helped
propel Vivien into a business that typically includes 22 to

Published in 1977, *A Very Young Rider* brought readers
into the life of 10-year-old Vivi Malloy.

24 horses, from foals to racing age. She runs horses from
Florida to New York with several trainers and is on the
board of directors for the New York Breeders Association.

"It's my passion, and I love it," she said. "I'm also
involved in open-space and conservation associations, which
goes with the riding, breeding and hunting—it all goes
together."

Vivien's oldest daughter, Debby, 17 when the book was
written, went on to continue her riding career and still
competes on the European show jumping circuit.

She married legendary German show jumper Hans-
Günter Winkler, who won four Olympic team gold medals,
one individual Olympic gold and two consecutive World
Championships (1954 and '55) with the legendary mare
Halla.

Now 46, Debby Winkler is campaigning several horses at
the grand prix level. Earlier this year, her Sakrus HG placed
sixth in the qualifier for the grand prix at the Spangenburg
(Germany) CSI***, and she also rode two other horses—
San Orcano and Sunrise 46—to ribbons in the 1.40-meter
classes there.

Debby specializes in starting young horses and often
markets them to riders and trainer in North America,

Vivi and Mark Malloy, with Ready Penny and Casey respectfully,
enjoyed success in Pony Club. As C-1 members of the Greenwich
Team they won the Regional Rally in 1975.